TREASURY OF BIBLE STORIES

Table of Contents
Old Testament Stories

Table of Contents
New Testament Stories

GOD
MADE THE WORLD

Retold by Dandi

Before the beginning,
There was no blue sky.
No plants and no people,
And nothing to buy!

Then God said the word.

He said, *"Let there be light!"*

And out of pure nothing,

God made day and night!

Next, God made the heavens
Of marvelous worth.
And held back the waters
To form the dry earth.

God saw what He did
And said, *"That's pretty good."*
Then followed with flowers
As only God could.

"We're going to need seasons,
And then just for fun,
I'll whip up a moon
And I'll throw in a sun."

Then next came a robin,
A finch, a bluebird,
And beautiful peacocks,
When God gave the word.

19

And then God decided
To fill up the seas,
With fishes and dolphins
And whales, if you please.

"Well, all that's not bad,"
Said the Lord, *"but there's more."*
So God made some ducks
And more beasts than before.

Then on came the camels
And horses and dogs,
The lions, the zebras,
And don't forget frogs.

"But still I'm not done yet.
There's more to my plan."
And out of the dust
God created a man.

"I've saved this for last,
And these last are my best."
And God made a woman.
Then God took a rest.

Our God must be great!

Now you know that it's true.

God made all the world,

And He made it for YOU!

The Story of
NOAH

Retold by Dandi

Long, long ago the people of the earth turned their backs on God. They hurt each other so much, it broke God's heart. If God told the people to do one thing, they tried to come up with a plan to do just the opposite. Everybody disobeyed God – except for one man.

Noah loved God with all his heart. Even though everybody around him did mean, rotten things, Noah was kind and good. When God told Noah to do something, Noah did it. That's what made him happy.

Noah did all he could to raise his family according to God's commands. "God always keeps His promises," Noah told his sons, Shem, Ham, and Japheth, time and time again.

One day God spoke to Noah. "Noah, I'm going to cover the earth with water in a worldwide flood. But I'm making you a promise. I'll keep you and your family safe."

Then God told Noah to build a giant boat, an ark, made out of wood. Noah had trouble picturing what an ark would look like because he had never seen one. God gave him all the details. "You'll have to make rooms and stalls; an upper, middle, and lower deck; windows, and a door in the side of the ark."

Noah did everything just as God commanded.

So Noah set about building the ark.

"What are you building, Noah?" asked his neighbors.

"God told me to build an ark," said Noah. "And that's just what I'm doing."

"An ark?" said one bearded man, scoffing. "In the desert? You're crazy!"

"God is sending a flood to cover the whole earth," Noah said, hammering a spike into a board.

"A flood?" Then all the people burst out laughing.

Years went by with no rain. More years passed. People came from miles around to laugh at Noah and his ark. But Noah knew God always keeps His promises. So he did everything God commanded him to.

41

Finally Noah finished the ark.

God said, "Noah, it's time to gather the animals, a pair of every kind of beast and fish and bird. One week from today, I will bring the rains."

So Noah brought the animals to the ark – a boy and a girl of every kind of creature. Two by two, the animals marched up the ramp and into the ark.

Noah did everything that God commanded him to.

"It's time," Noah told his family. Just as soon as Noah, his wife, his sons and their wives boarded the ark, God slammed the door of the ark shut!

Noah listened. Above the gentle moo of the cows and the quacks of the ducks, Noah thought he heard something. First, a plink, plunk. Then a rat-a-tat. Then a clatter as rain struck the earth with violent force.

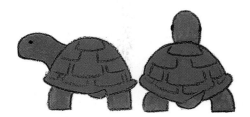

For forty days and nights it rained and poured. Noah and his family were safe inside the ark. Noah felt the ark lift higher and higher as the waters rose above the trees, above the mountains.

After forty days, Noah listened, but he no longer heard the pinging on the roof of the ark. The rain had stopped. For five more months the ark floated, until it came to rest on top of Mt. Ararat. Months later Noah looked out the window over the vast waters. He could see the tops of the mountains poking through.

"I'll send out a bird," Noah said. He chose a dove, a timid, little bird of peace. "If she finds dry land, she will stay away. Then we will know the earth has dried," he said.

Out flew the little dove. But she found no dry land and returned to the ark. A week later Noah sent the dove again in search of dry land. That night, the dove returned, but this time Noah saw she had something in her mouth. An olive leaf! Noah knew now that the dove had found a tree. The land was becoming dry!

When Noah sent the dove out a week later, he was not surprised that she failed to return. The dove had found dry land and was making her nest in an olive tree!

"It's time to come out, Noah," God told him.

Noah opened the door. Out flew the birds, two by two. Carefully, the animals walked down the ramp in pairs, kicking up their heels when they set foot on dry land.

Last out of the ark came Noah and his family. They praised God for the sunshine on their faces and the dry land and fresh grass at their feet. They thanked God for always keeping His promises.

Then God said, "Look up in the clouds!"

Noah looked up at the most beautiful arc of colors — a rainbow!

"This is a sign of my promise to you," God said. "When it appears in the sky, I will look down on the rainbow and remember my promise to never again flood the whole world."

So when you see a rainbow, remember that God is looking from the other side of that rainbow. It is His promise to you forever.

JOSEPH
AND
THE VERY COLORFUL COAT
Retold by Andy Rector

Illustrated by Donna Lee Hill

Jacob had twelve sons. Some were big and strong. Some were skinny. Some had brown hair. Some had black hair. Some had long beards. Some had short beards. Some did not have a beard at all. Of all his sons, however, Jacob's favorite was Joseph.

Joseph and his brothers helped their father by watching the flocks of sheep. They made sure that none of the sheep wandered off. They protected the sheep from lions and bears. If a sheep cut itself on a rock, they would rub oil on the wound to help heal the sheep.

Joseph loved to play with the lambs. By watching his older brothers, Joseph learned how to take care of the sheep.

Because Joseph was his father's favorite, Jacob gave him a present.

"Joseph," said Jacob one day, "I have something for you."

"What is it, Father?" asked Joseph.

Jacob handed Joseph a bundle of cloth. Joseph unfolded the cloth. "It's a coat!" said Joseph. "And it's so colorful. Thank you, Father."

Joseph put on his colorful new coat and ran off to find his brothers.

"Look at my new coat!"

"Where did you get it?" they asked.

"From Father," said Joseph. He turned around to show the coat's beautiful colors.

The brothers grumbled among themselves. "Joseph thinks he's better than us because of that coat."

Later that night Joseph told his brothers about a dream he had. "The sun and moon and eleven stars bowed down to me," he said.

Joseph's brothers figured out that the sun represented their father, the moon represented their mother, and the eleven stars represented eleven brothers.

"So you're saying," said one of the brothers, "that your whole family should bow down to you?" This made the brothers even more angry.

Jacob walked up to Joseph one day and said, "Joseph go find your brothers. They are out in the countryside taking care of the sheep. Ask them how they are doing and if they need anything. Then come back to me and tell me what they say."

Joseph ran down the road to do what his father said.

"Here comes the dreamer!" said one of the brothers.

"What does he want?" said another. "Look at him. He thinks he is so wonderful."

The brothers huddled together. "Let's kill him."

"No!" said Reuben, the oldest brother. "Let's not kill him. Let's throw him in that deep hole instead."

The brothers ripped the fancy coat off of Joseph and threw him in a deep hole.

"That will teach him to mess with us," they said.

Reuben planned to rescue Joseph at a later time, so he went out to the fields to watch the sheep and wait.

Joseph cried out from the deep hole. "Help! Why have you done this? Help!" But his brothers only laughed at him.

Joseph wrapped his arms around his body and shivered. The hole was dark, damp, and cold.

Soon a caravan of traveling merchants passed nearby.

"I have an idea," said one of the brothers. "Let's sell Joseph as a slave to the caravan. We might as well make a little money out of all this." The other brothers agreed.

So they lifted Joseph out of the hole and sold him to the caravan. Off traveled Joseph with the merchants and the camels.

When Reuben returned from the fields, he looked into the hole and saw Joseph missing.

"Where is Joseph?" Reuben asked.

"We sold him to a caravan," said the brothers. "He's going to be a slave."

All the brothers except Reuben laughed loud and long.

Later the brothers realized that they had to give their father a reason for Joseph's disappearance. "What are we going to tell him?" they asked each other.

The brothers came up with a plan. They took Joseph's robe and dipped it in the blood of an animal.

Then they all went back home and into the tent of their father.

"Where is Joseph?" Jacob asked, noticing that his youngest son was missing.

"Well, Father," one of the brothers explained, "we have something to tell you."

"We found this, Father." They handed Jacob the coat that had been stained in blood.

"Some ferocious animal must have killed Joseph!" said Jacob. Jacob began to cry. Even though they were angry with their father for picking Joseph as his favorite, the brothers felt ashamed for what they had done.

Slowly, one by one, they walked out of the tent in silence. They stared at the ground in shame. Even Reuben did not tell their father what had really happened.

"Joseph, Joseph," cried Jacob. "I will always miss you."

Jacob stayed sad for a long time.

Many years passed. One year food was scarce because the sky would not rain. Fields dried up. Streams dried up. Animals starved.

"Go to Egypt, my sons," said Jacob. "I hear there is food there."

So the brothers all headed for Egypt.

When they arrived in Egypt, a man stood before them. This man had almost as much power as the King of Egypt.

"It's me–Joseph!" said the man.

"Joseph!" cried the brothers. When they saw that he had risen from being a slave to becoming a powerful ruler, they were afraid of him.

"I forgive you," said Joseph.

From then on, the brothers treated Joseph with kindness.

THE STORY OF
JOSEPH
in EGYPT

Retold by ANDY RECTOR

Illustrated by Ben Mahan

81

"This strong young man would make an excellent servant," said the slave trader. "Who would like to buy him?"

Soon Joseph found himself walking down the street with a man named Potiphar. "I need you to help feed and clean the animals, Joseph," said Potiphar. "You will help my other servants pick grain in the fields and clean the house. We will take care of you."

As Joseph grew older, he proved to be a good servant. Potiphar liked Joseph so much, he put Joseph in charge of his whole household.

The Pharaoh, king of Egypt, became angry with his cupbearer and his baker. Pharaoh threw them into prison. One night the cupbearer and the baker each had a dream. The next morning Joseph walked by them as they sat in jail and saw frowns on their faces.

"I had a strange dream," said the cupbearer.

"Tell me about your dream," said Joseph.

"I saw a vine with three branches of grapes," said the cupbearer. "I squeezed the grapes into a cup I held and a cup the Pharaoh held."

"The three branches," said Joseph, "means three days. Pharaoh will restore you as his cupbearer in three days."

Then the baker told Joseph his dream. "That is not a good dream," said Joseph.

The Lord helped Joseph know what the dream meant. In three days, what Joseph had said earlier happened. Pharaoh restored the cupbearer to his position. The baker was not so lucky.

One night Pharaoh woke up from a disturbing dream. He told his dream to the magicians and wise men, but none of them understood it.

"Wait," said the cupbearer, "When I was in prison I met a man named Joseph who could understand dreams."

"Get him," said Pharaoh.

Soon Joseph stood before Pharaoh. "In my dream, Joseph, I saw seven healthy cows grazing along the river. Suddenly seven sickly and scrawny cows came out of the river and ate up the seven healthy cows. Can you understand this dream, Joseph?"

"God helps me to understand dreams," said Joseph. "The seven healthy cows mean seven years of a lot of food and grain. The seven sickly cows mean seven years of famine and very little food. Egypt will have seven years of good crops followed by seven years of famine. You should save some food from the good years and use it during the bad years."

Pharaoh was amazed at Joseph's wisdom. "God has made you wise. I am putting you in charge of my palace, Joseph. No one will have more power in Egypt than you, except for me."

During the following seven years, Joseph had grain stored in barns. After seven years the famine began, but the Egyptians had plenty of food. The Lord watched over Joseph and helped save Egypt from the famine.

MOSES
AND
THE VERY SPECIAL BASKET

retold by Andy Rector

Illustrated by Linda Welty

The Pharaoh ruled as king over Egypt. The Israelites served as slaves for Pharaoh. One day he looked out his palace window. He saw Israelites making bricks, carrying rocks, and picking grain.

"There are too many Israelite slaves," said the Pharaoh. "They might get ideas about fighting against Egypt to escape slavery."

So the Pharaoh made a law: when an Israelite baby boy was born, he was to be killed.

Soon after Pharaoh made the law, one Israelite woman gave birth to a baby boy. "I must do something to save my baby boy's life," said the mother.

The mother and her daughter, Miriam, prayed to the Lord for help.

Then the mother came up with a plan. "Miriam," said the mother to the baby's older sister, "Help me weave a basket."

When they finished the basket, the mother spread tar and pitch on it to make it waterproof.

"What are you going to do?" asked Miriam.

"You'll see," said the mother.

Down by the river the mother and Miriam carried the baby and the basket. Miriam lay the baby in the basket.

With a push, the mother sent her baby boy floating away in the basket.

"Follow your brother," said the mother. "See what happens."

The basket floated down, down, down the river. The current carried the baby boy away. But Miriam followed behind. She hid among the cattails and the lily pads.

Suddenly Miriam heard splashing and laughter nearby.

Miram spied girls along the river bank. "That one girl must be a princess -- Pharaoh's daughter," thought Miriam.

The princess had walked down to the river to bathe. Her maid servants were helping her. Suddenly the princess saw the basket.

"What is that?" asked the princess.

"I don't know," said one of the maid servants. "I'll go get it."

"It's a baby!" said the princess. "An Israelite baby!"

"Why is he floating in a basket on the river?" asked one of the maid servants.

"I don't know," said the princess. "But I do know that my father has made a law. All Israelite baby boys are to be killed at birth."

"If your father sees this baby," said one of the maid servants, "he'll have him killed!"

"Yes," the princess said. "But I can't bear to think of anything happening to this beautiful baby.

The princess lifted the baby out of the basket. She hugged him.

"I want to keep the baby," said the princess. "I will raise him as my son."

"We can't tell your father that he is an Israelite baby," said a maid servant.

"I know," said the princess. "We'll say it's an Egyptian baby that I adopted."

Miriam became frightened. "What will happen to my baby brother?" she thought.

With loud splashing, Miriam ran through the water and up to the princess. "I know an Israelite woman who will help you take care of the baby," said Miriam.

"Yes, that is a good idea," the princess said. "Go get her."

Miriam rushed back to get her mother.

"Mother!" said Miriam, "The Pharaoh's daughter wants to adopt the baby! And she needs our help to take care of him."

"Thank you, Lord," said the mother. She knew if the princess adopted the baby, he would be safe.

Miriam grabbed her mother's hand. "This way," said Miriam.

They waded through the water and ran along the bank of the river until they found the princess.

"Please take care of this baby," said the princess. "I will pay you for it. When he gets a little older, bring him back to the palace and I will raise him as my son."

The mother and Miriam took the baby boy back home.

"God answered our prayers," said the mother. "We asked Him to help us find a way to protect the baby, and He did."

Miriam held her baby brother close to her cheek. She kissed his forehead. "Thank you, God," she whispered.

That night the mother rocked her baby to sleep. "The princess will make sure that the Pharaoh won't harm my baby."

One day soon, the mother would have to take the baby to the palace to live with the princess. She did not mind, because her baby would be safe.

When the baby went to live in the palace, the princess named him Moses. Moses became a great leader of the Israelite people and led them out of slavery from Egypt.

MOSES LEADS THE LORD'S PEOPLE

Retold by Andy Rector

Illustrated by Ben Mahan

One day Moses took a flock of sheep on a hillside. He saw a bush on the hillside burning, but the leaves and branches did not turn black and crumble to ashes. They remained green and alive. "How strange," thought Moses. "I am going over to get a closer look at this bush."

"Moses! Moses!"

"Who said that?" asked Moses. He heard the voice calling him but did not see anyone else.

"I am God. The Hebrews are slaves to the Egyptians. They suffer much. You, Moses, are a Hebrew. I want you to go back to Egypt and talk to the Pharaoh. Tell him to free the Hebrews from slavery. I have a new land for them, a land flowing with milk and honey."

One day Moses visited Pharaoh. "The Lord demands that you let his people go or the Nile will turn into blood." Pharaoh refused and so the Nile turned into red blood. The fish died and the air smelled bad.

Moses went to Pharaoh again. "The Lord demands that you let his people go or He will plague your country with frogs." Pharaoh refused and so frogs appeared everywhere.

Moses went to Pharaoh again. "The Lord demands that you let his people go or He will plague your country with gnats." Pharaoh refused and so gnats appeared everywhere.

Moses went to Pharaoh again. "The Lord demands that you let his people go or He will plague your country with flies." Pharaoh refused and so flies appeared everywhere.

The Lord continued to plague Egypt. Moses would warn Pharaoh, but Pharaoh's heart remained hardened. The Lord caused the livestock to be sick. He put boils on the Egyptians. He sent a hailstorm that destroyed the crops of the Egyptians. He caused a swarm of locust to eat what was left of the crops after the hailstorm. He caused darkness to cover the land for three days. Still Pharaoh would not let the Hebrews leave.

Moses went to Pharaoh again. "The Lord demands that you let his people go or the firstborn son of each Egyptian family will die." Pharaoh refused. At midnight the firstborn son of every Egyptian family died. Even the

Pharaoh's son died.

He finally decided to let all the Hebrews leave.

The Hebrews quickly left Egypt and headed for the land that God had promised them. Moses led the Hebrew people forward. They came to a sea. "How are we going to get across the sea?" They cried.

"The Lord is with us," said Moses. He stretched his staff over the waters of the sea. Suddenly the waters divided and formed a pathway of dry land for them to walk to the other side.

Soon the Hebrews reached the other side of the sea. After they were all safely across, the walls of water collapsed.

The Hebrews saw the Lord had saved them from the Egyptian Pharaoh. They trusted Moses and sang songs to honor the Lord.

JOSHUA LEADS THE HEBREWS AGAINST JERICHO

Retold by Andy Rector

Illustrated by Ben Mahan

After leading the Lord's people out of Egypt, Moses died. The Lord chose Joshua to lead the people, now called Israelites, into the promised land. "Be strong and courageous, Joshua," said the Lord. "The land I promised you is full of people who do not believe in me and would try to destroy you. I will protect you and my people."

Joshua gathered all the people together. "Do not be afraid of the strange land and the city called Jericho the Lord has given to us. He will protect us. Remember the promise he gave to Moses long ago."

The Israelites cheered Joshua. "We will be strong and courageous," they cried.

Joshua sent two spies into the city of Jericho. They went into a house of a woman named Rahab. They hid and rested in Rahab's house for the night.

The king of Jericho knew that the Israelites traveled near his city. "They want to take over Jericho!" He found out about the spies Joshua sent. He sent messengers to the house of Rahab. She covered the spies with stalks of a plant called flax. Then she told the messengers that the spies had already left.

After she closed the door, Rahab ran to where she had hidden the spies. "They're gone!" she said. The spies lifted off stalks of flax. "Thank you," they said, "You will be kept safe when our people return to take over the city."

To get into the promised land, the Israelites had to cross the Jordan River. The river had flooded the banks. "How are we going to get across?" the people asked.

"Trust the Lord," said Joshua. "He will help us get into the promised land." Then Joshua had some men pick up the Ark of the Covenant -- a large gold box that contained the spirit of the Lord. They carried the Ark to the bank of the river. The river stopped flowing and soon, dry land appeared. A path formed where the river had been. The men carrying the Ark walked into the middle of the dry riverbed and stood. All the Israelites crossed the Jordan River.

After everyone had crossed, Joshua said, "Come up out of the Jordan." The men carrying the Ark finished crossing the riverbed to the other side. Soon the water began to flow again.

Joshua and his army marched around Jericho seven times. After the seventh time around, Joshua said to the people, "Shout! The Lord is giving you this city!"

The trumpets blared and the people shouted. The walls of Jericho crumbled to the ground.

Joshua said to the two spies, "Quick, go in and get Rahab and her family out of Jericho." The spies rushed in and brought out Rahab and her family. They took Rahab to a safe place, just as they had promised. Soon Israel had control of the city.

The people trusted the Lord and worshipped Him for helping give them the land.

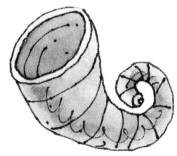

SAMSON HELPS
HIS PEOPLE

Retold by Andy Rector

Illustrated by Ben Mahan

One day a man appeared to Manoah, an Israelite, and his wife.

"You are going to have a son," said the man. "He will be special and will be used by the Lord. He is never to get a haircut or drink wine and he must eat special foods."

The man vanished and Manoah realized the man was an angel of God.

Soon the woman gave birth to a son and named him Samson.

"Mother," said Samson as a boy. "Why can't I eat the foods the other boys eat?"

"God has made you special," said Samson's mother.

"The other children make fun of me," Samson said, "because my hair is so long. When can I get it cut?"

"The Lord has instructed us to never cut your hair," was all his mother would say.

The Spirit of the Lord filled Samson. He grew up into a strong man. Many times he fought the Philistines -- the enemies of the Israelites. One time the Philistines tricked him and the Spirit of the Lord gave Samson the strength to kill thirty of them.

"What have you done?" said Samson's fellow Israelites. "Don't you know that the Philistines are our enemies? Now they will be more mad at us than ever!"

"Tie me up and hand me over to the Philistines," said Samson. "I will make everything all right."

The Israelites tied up Samson and handed him over to the Philistines. Suddenly the ropes that bound Samson dropped to the ground. He picked up a jawbone of a donkey laying on the ground nearby. With that jawbone he fought a one-man war against the Philistines. Before Samson had finished, he had slain one thousand Philistines.

One day Samson fell in love with a Philistine woman named Delilah. Delilah could not be trusted. The leaders of the Philistines met her one day and said, "See if you can find out the secret of his strength."

So Delilah asked Samson, "What is the secret of your strength?"

"If you tie me up with new ropes, I'm helpless," said Samson.

So Delilah tied him up with new ropes. The Philistines tried to attack Samson, but he broke out of the ropes with no problem.

"You lied!" cried Delilah. "I won't love you anymore if you don't tell me your secret."

"Then here is my secret," said Samson. "If my hair is cut, my strength will leave me."

One day Samson rested his head in Delilah's lap. "I'm going to take a nap."

A Philistine man sneaked into the room and cut off Samson's hair.

"The Philistines are going to get you!" cried Delilah.

Samson awoke and found his hair cut off and his strength gone. The Philistines tied him up and threw him in prison.

The Philistines made noise and danced. They ate food and drank wine. About three thousand Philistines gathered in the temple. "Bring out Samson," they cried. They wanted to make fun of him.

Samson asked the servant leading him, "Please place me between two tall pillars in the temple."

Samson prayed to the Lord. "God forgive me for telling my secret. Please give me my strength back."

Suddenly the Spirit of the Lord filled Samson. He pushed the two pillars and the whole temple caved in, killing the Philistines inside as well as himself.

RUTH and NAOMI HELP EACH OTHER

Retold by Andy Rector

Illustrated by Ben Mahan

A famine scorched the land called Judah. "Let's move to the land of Moab," said Elimelech. "There is food in Moab." So Elimelech packed up all his possessions, and he and his family traveled to Moab. Elimelech and his family worshipped God. They knew He would protect them.

"We will live here in Moab," said Elimelech. Naomi, his wife, and their sons unpacked and settled in the land of Moab.

Over the years, Naomi watched her two sons grow into fine young men. Each son found a wife among the Moabite people and married them.

One day Elimelech died. Soon both of Naomi's son's died. Naomi talked with Ruth and Orpah, her daughters-in-law.

"Our husbands are dead," said Naomi. "I am going back to Judah."

"I think it would be best if you two returned to your mothers' houses and live there until you marry again."

"We don't want to leave you!" cried the women.

"It's for the best," said Naomi.

So Orpah sadly kissed her mother-in-law good-bye. Ruth, however, stayed.

"I can't leave you by yourself," said Ruth. "Where you go, I will go. Where you stay, I will stay. Your people will be my people and your God my God."

So Naomi and Ruth traveled back to Judah to the town of Bethlehem.

After arriving in Judah, Naomi saw a man working with his servant in the fields.

"That man is Boaz. He is a distant relative of mine," said Naomi to Ruth. "See if you can meet him. Maybe if he likes you, he might marry you one day."

So Ruth began working with the servants in the field of Boaz. She worked hard all day.

"Who is that woman?" Boaz asked one of his servants.

"I talked to her earlier," said the servant. "She came back with your relative, Naomi. Her name is Ruth and she is from Moab."

Boaz walked up to Ruth. "Hello. Thank you for helping me. If you get thirsty there is water in jars over there."

"Thank you," said Ruth.

"Just follow the girl servants and do what they do. And don't let the men servants bother you. They can be rough sometimes."

"Thank you so much for showing me kindness."

Soon Ruth and Boaz fell in love. One day he married Ruth and took care of her and Naomi. Ruth and Boaz had a son named Obed. Obed grew up and had a son named Jesse. When Jesse grew up he had seven sons, one of whom became King David. Yes, Ruth was the great grandmother of King David.

DAVID
AND
THE VERY SCARY GIANT
Retold by Andy Rector

Illustrated by Donna Lee Hill

David watched his older brothers march down the road. They were soldiers in the army of Israel. The Israelites and the Philistines fought each other. David waved good-bye.

"I want to help them," said David.

"You aren't old enough to fight in the war," said Jesse, David's father.

"I need you to help me here at home," said Jesse. "Why don't you watch the sheep while your brothers are gone?"

So David walked out to the fields to take care of the sheep.

Sometimes the sheep got in trouble. David helped them. He chased off wild animals like bears and lions that wanted to hurt the sheep. He picked them up when they fell off of steep ledges. He rubbed oil on their hurts when the sheep cut themselves. Watching the sheep kept David busy.

Day after day passed, but David did not get bored. He always brought his harp to play music. David plucked the strings of the harp and sang songs about God and the beautiful world He created.

The sheep liked to listen to David sing. When they heard him sing, they knew he sat nearby. That made the sheep feel safe.

Even though David spent many hours and days out in the field watching the sheep, he did not feel lonely. He had his friends, the sheep, to keep him company.

But David also had a special friend to keep him company. This friend was God. Everyday after David sang songs to God, he prayed to Him.

David watched over the sheep at night. They knew he would protect them from wild animals, find them if they got lost, and help them if they got hurt.

At night, David knew God watched over him. David knew God was with him at all times.

One day Jesse asked David to take food to his brothers at the army campsite. David put on his shepherd's bag and then ran down the road carrying bread and cheese for his older brothers to eat.

"This is from Father," said David when he arrived at the tents. He handed the food to his brothers.

"Thank you, David," they said.

Across the valley from where Israel's army camped, the other army -- the Philistines -- stood and watched. Standing taller than any other Philistine man, was Goliath. From the bottom of his feet to the top of his head, Goliath measured nine feet tall.

"Come on, you puny Israelites," yelled Goliath across the valley. "We've been out here for days. Let's fight and get this over with."

Even from across the valley, David could see that Goliath stood as tall as a giant. David, however, did not fear Goliath because he knew that God stood bigger than anyone.

David looked at his brothers and the other Israelite soldiers. He saw their eyes open wide and their knees shake.

"Why are you afraid of Goliath?" said David.

"I dare one of you to fight me," yelled Goliath from across the valley.

David saw the Philistines laughing and pointing their fingers at the Israelite army. "Isn't anyone going to challenge him?" asked David.

175

David tried to wear the armor of the Israelite soldiers. "This is too big for me," he said. "I'm not use to this armor."

So instead David looked at the only weapon he had -- a slingshot -- and thought of a plan.

David walked over to a brook of water and looked around. "Here we are," said David. He used his staff to pull out five smooth stones from the brook. He placed the stones in his shepherd's bag.

By this time no one had yet challenged Goliath. David walked over to the giant Philistine.

"Where are you going?" shouted David's brothers.

"I am not afraid," said David. "God will help me."

"Who is this 'God?'" said Goliath. The giant began laughing. "And who is this small boy that the Israelites have sent over to fight for them?"

David swung his slingshot around and around.

Goliath yelled, "If you think a little rock will hurt me, you'd better try harder."

David let the stone soar through the air. With a loud thud, the stone smacked the giant right in the middle of his forehead. Goliath's shoulders sagged and then he fell to the ground -- dead. The Philistine soldiers saw this and ran away.

The Israelites called David a hero. From that day, David served in the Israelite army.

WISE SOLOMON LEADS THE PEOPLE

Retold by Andy Rector

Illustrated by Ben Mahan

David -- the David who played the harp, tended the sheep, and fought Goliath -- became king of Israel. He ruled many years. When he died, his son, Solomon, became king.

One night God appeared to Solomon. "Ask for whatever you want and I will give it to you."

Solomon thought for a moment and then said, "Lord, give me wisdom and knowledge, so I can be a good king to the people of Israel."

"Since you asked for wisdom," said the Lord, "and not something selfish like long life or untold riches, I will give you knowledge and wisdom. I will also make you richer than any king who has ever lived or ever will live."

Over the years, Solomon acquired great wealth as King. He had chariots and soldiers. He had servants and dancers and cooks. He had money and jewels that filled rooms. He lived in a beautiful palace and built many large buildings. He also built many gardens with lovely plants and trees.

Solomon arranged for the building of a temple for the Lord. Thousands of workers spent years building the walls and making pieces of furniture for the Lord's temple. After the workers finished building the temple, the Israelites gathered around it and celebrated.

Solomon used his wisdom to write books that have lasted until this day. One of those books is called Proverbs. These proverbs can be found in the Bible.

A proverb is a short saying with a big message. He wrote many proverbs about friendship: "A friend sticks closer than a brother . . . As iron sharpens iron, so one man sharpens another."

Solomon wrote about wealth and true happiness: "Better a poor man in a happy house than a rich man in a house full of arguing."

He also wrote about obeying the Lord: "The man who respects God is blessed, but the man with a hard heart toward God is in trouble."

One day two women stood before Solomon.

"This woman stole my baby because hers died!" said one woman. "She switched her dead baby with my live one."

"No!" screamed the other woman. "Your baby died and this is mine."

Solomon held a sword over the baby. "I will cut the baby in half, and give one half to one woman and the other half to the other woman."

One woman said, "Please don't kill him! He is my baby." She pleaded and cried.

The other woman said, "Go ahead. Cut him in half and kill him. Then neither one of us will have him."

Solomon knew from the reaction of the women that the one who pleaded and cried was the real mother.

Everyone who saw this incident was amazed. They knew that Solomon had wisdom from God.

ESTHER
THE
VERY BRAVE QUEEN

Retold by Andy Rector

Illustrated by Andra Chase

Esther lived with her cousin Mordecai. They were Jews. Esther's parents had died when she was a child. Mordecai had raised her. Esther thought of Mordecai as more of a father than a cousin.

Esther and Mordecai lived in a time and in a land where a king named Xerxes ruled. Everyone obeyed Xerxes. Whatever he wanted he got.

Xerxes had a rule: No one could approach his throne to talk to him unless he first asked you to do so. Anyone who approached the throne without first asking was put to death.

However, if someone did approach the throne without being asked and the king waved his golden scepter, the person's life would be spared.

"I need a wife," said King Xerxes one day. "Bring to me all the beautiful women of the land."

A search followed. When the king's helpers saw Esther, they said, "She is so beautiful! She must be shown to the king."

Esther packed her bags. She was excited about the idea of being the wife of a king, but she was nervous too.

"This is so exciting, Cousin Mordecai," said Esther.

"There is something I should say," said Mordecai. "Remember this: don't tell anyone you are a Jew."

"Why?" asked Esther.

"Some people do not understand us," said Mordecai.

"I won't tell anyone," said Esther.

So they took Esther to the palace with all the other most beautiful women of the land. All the women were given beautiful dresses and jewelry to wear. People from the palace styled their hair.

Esther looked around at all the women. "With all these beautiful women," thought Esther to herself, "I wonder who will be chosen as the king's wife?"

The king saw all the women, but something about Esther made him love her above the others.

"She is beautiful not only on the outside," said King Xerxes, "but on the inside as well."

Esther could not believe it. "The king has chosen me!" she said.

Soon a wedding followed. Esther became the wife of King Xerxes. As the wife of a king, Esther also became a queen. King Xerxes had a beautiful crown made for Esther.

Mordecai attended the wedding ceremony. He was pleased for her. He did wonder, however, if Esther would remember not to tell anyone she was a Jew.

King Xerxes had a helper named Haman. Haman walked around the streets of the land with his head up in the air. He thought he was important. "I work for the king," he told people. "You must do what I say." People bowed down to Haman.

One day Haman walked down the street. As usual, everyone bowed down to him -- except for one man -- Mordecai.

"Who was that man?" asked Haman. Someone told him that his name was Mordecai and that he was a Jew.

"Hmmm," said Haman. A plan came to Haman's mind.

"King Xerxes," said Haman, "There is a group of people who live in your kingdom who do not respect you."

"What?" said King Xerxes. "Who are these people?"

"They are the Jews," said Haman. "They do things differently than you or I. It's not good to have them in your kingdom. They should be destroyed."

"Very well," said the king as he signed a new law that declared all the Jews to be killed. "Haman, you are in charge of making sure this law is obeyed."

The law was read throughout the land. The Jews became upset. When Mordecai heard about the new law, he sent a message to Esther at the palace.

"Oh, no," said Esther after reading Mordecai's message. "The king does not know that I am a Jew. I must talk to him and save my people."

Even though Esther was the Queen, she could not approach the throne unless the king waved his golden scepter at her. She walked up to the king. "I have to ask you something," she said.

King Xerxes waved his golden scepter at Esther. "Yes, my queen. What is it you want? I would give you half of my kingdom if you wished."

"Thank you, my king," said Esther. "But I only wish to have dinner with you and Haman tomorrow night. At dinner I will tell you what I want."

"I accept," said King Xerxes.

The next evening King Xerxes, Queen Esther, and Haman sat down for dinner.

"Delicious," said the king to Esther. "Now tell me what it is you want. You know I would give you half of my kingdom."

"My king," said Esther, "a law has been passed in the land that says my people should be killed."

"Who, would allow such a law that would harm my queen?" asked the king. He was angry.

"Haman came up with the idea," said Esther. "The people to be killed are the Jews. I am a Jew."

The king changed the law. "If anyone attacks the Jews," said the king, "they are allowed to defend themselves."

He also sentenced Haman to death.

Soon word spread through the land that Esther risked her life by visiting the king without being asked first.

"Hooray for Esther!" cried the Jews. "She saved us!"

King Xerxes declared a holiday for the Jews. "Every year at this time you should remember how you were saved," said the king. To this day Jewish people celebrate Purim to remember what Esther did for them.

The Story of
DANIEL

Retold by Dandi

Daniel loved God with all his heart. He always did his best, and so became the chief helper to King Darius.

"Daniel," said the king. "Of all my governors and helpers, you give the best advice. You work the hardest and rule more fairly than all the rest. I'm thinking of putting you in charge of the whole empire."

When the other governors and rulers saw how well Daniel ruled, they grew jealous. "Daniel did this. Daniel said that!" complained one governor.

"King Darius likes Daniel best!" said a second governor.

Then they had an idea. "Let's spy on Daniel! Surely we can find something Daniel has done wrong!"

But when they met back together, not one of them could find anything to criticize Daniel for! Daniel had never lied to or cheated anybody!

"Since we can't find any law Daniel has broken," said one ruler, "we will have to get the king to make a new law."

"Daniel would never break a law," said the wicked governor, "unless we make up a law against Daniel's God."

So the governors paid a visit to the king. "Oh, great King Darius, we have come up with a new law. If anyone prays to God or man – except to you – during the next thirty days, he should be thrown into a den of lions. Now all you have to do is sign the law."

"Hmm..." puzzled the king absently. So King Darius signed the new law.

Daniel heard about the new law forbidding anyone to pray to God. He knew King Darius couldn't change the law once he'd signed it. But Daniel also knew he could never stop praying to God. So just as he had always done, Daniel knelt beside his window and prayed.

Outside the window lurked the jealous governors. As soon as they heard Daniel pray, they jumped up. "That's it!" they cried. "Now we tell the king!"

The governors ran as fast as they could to the palace. "King Darius, Daniel broke your law and prayed to God. You have no choice but to arrest him and throw him to the lions!"

King Darius loved Daniel, but he couldn't take back his word. With a broken heart, he sent a guard for Daniel. Hungry lions roared as Daniel was taken to the pit and thrown to the lions! "Daniel, I hope your God can save you," cried King Darius.

Daniel landed on his back, smack in the middle of the lions' den. He opened his eyes to see sharp fangs glaring at him from the mouths of hungry lions.

"Time to pray," said Daniel. "Lord," he prayed, "you have always taken care of me. I trust you now."

When Daniel opened his eyes, he no longer saw fangs! All the lions had their mouths shut! In the middle of the lions' den, Daniel saw a shining angel above the lions. God had sent His angel to take care of Daniel!

King Darius didn't eat or drink. He couldn't sleep the whole night, worrying about Daniel. Very early in the morning, Darius jumped up and ran to the lions' den.

"Daniel!" cried the king. "I know you serve the living God. Was your God able to save you from the lions?" Then King Darius held his breath and listened.

"King Darius," Daniel shouted up. "My God sent an angel to shut the lions' mouths." When he was pulled up, Daniel didn't have a scratch on him!

"Hallelujah!" shouted the king. "Send those wicked governors to the lions' den themselves!"

King Darius wrote a new law and sent it throughout the empire:

I decree that everyone in my empire should pray and honor the God of Daniel. His Kingdom will never be destroyed, and His power will never end! He protects His people and performs miracles. He delivered Daniel from the lions!

Daniel and King Darius were best friends from that day on. They were best friends with God, too, and talked to God about everything. No one in the kingdom ever forgot about Daniel, the lions' den, or Daniel's God.

The Story of
JONAH

Retold by Dandi

"JONAH!"

Jonah looked around, but saw no one. Then he knew. The Lord God was calling him!

"Jonah!" God said again. "I want you to go to Nineveh."

'Nineveh?!' thought Jonah. 'Not there! Anywhere but there.'

"Jonah, you must warn the people of Nineveh. Tell them to stop being so bad or something really bad will happen to them!"

Jonah thought about that. "Hmmm. I could go to Nineveh like God says. Or..."

"... On the other hand," Jonah reasoned, "what if the people of Nineveh don't want to hear about God? What if they take it out on me? And even if they listen to me and change their ways, what good is that to me? To tell the truth, I'd like to see them get what's coming to them!"

So Jonah made the wrong choice. He decided *not* to obey God. Instead of heading for Nineveh, Jonah set off to the sea in the opposite direction.

Jonah bought himself a ticket on a ship bound for Tarshish. He climbed aboard and watched as the sailors rowed the ship out to sea.

"Ah, this is more like it," Jonah said. "This old ship is the perfect hiding place. Surely God can't find me here. I'll get as far away from Nineveh as I can."

But Jonah was wrong. God blew a strong wind over the sea. The sails of the ship whipped and moaned. The boat creaked as it rocked in the water, tossed by the terrible storm. White crested waves dashed against the ship. Water splashed over the sides. The sailors struggled as raging waters threatened to pull them all to the bottom of the sea!

Jonah watched in silence as the desperate sailors shouted for help. They threw their baggage overboard to lighten the load and keep them from sinking.

"Do something!" one of the sailors screamed at Jonah. "We don't know who you are or where you come from, but if you have a God, pray! Ask Him to save us! Beg your God for mercy!"

Jonah knew without a doubt that God had sent the storm because of him. God was speaking to him – not with words this time, but with a storm.

"This is all my fault," Jonah admitted. "I worship the God who made the earth and sea. I'm on this ship because I'm running away from God."

"What should we do so your God will stop the storm?" asked the Captain.

"Throw me overboard into the sea!" declared Jonah.

None of the sailors wanted to throw Jonah overboard. They tried harder to row to safety, but nothing helped. Finally, with a prayer to God to forgive them, they did what Jonah asked.

"One, two, three!" They flung Jonah into the sea. And the storm stopped!

'Well, this is the end of me,' thought Jonah as he felt himself fall through the air to the sea below.

Plop! Jonah hit the water. Glub, glub...down he sank!

Just when Jonah could hold his breath no longer, he felt something swim up behind him! Suddenly he heard a GULP! He passed over teeth and tongue inside something very strange – but safe. Jonah realized with a start, he had been swallowed by a huge fish!

It was dark and smelly inside the big fish. For three days Jonah sat and thought, and thought, and thought. Finally, Jonah understood how much trouble he had put himself through by disobeying God – and how much trouble God had gone through to take care of him!

Jonah prayed, "Oh, Lord, I was silly to try to hide from you! You are with me even in the deepest ocean. You sent this huge fish to save me because you love me. I love you too! From now on I'll do whatever you say!"

What happened next made Jonah dizzy with laughter! Round and round the fish swam, with Jonah in his belly. When the fish got close to shore, he opened his huge mouth and spit Jonah right out onto dry land!

"I've got to be on my way," Jonah told the great fish. "You did your job. Now I must do mine!"

This time Jonah took the right road – straight to Nineveh! When he got there, Jonah told the people everything God had said. The people in Nineveh felt sorry for being so mean and bad. They prayed to God and asked for help. They promised to be better and obey Him.

Because of the message Jonah brought to Nineveh, their whole city was saved! From then on, the people of Nineveh worshiped God, who had brought Jonah out of the fish's mouth – to them.

MARY VISITS ELIZABETH

retold by Andy Rector

Illustrated by Ben Mahan

Zechariah entered the temple. As a priest, he had the duty of burning incense to the Lord. The people waited outside of the temple as Zechariah completed his duties. Suddenly an angel appeared to Zechariah.

"You and your wife Elizabeth have no children," said the angel, "but the Lord has told me to tell you that you and Elizabeth will have a son."

"But we are old," said Zechariah. "How is that possible?"

"I am Gabriel," said the angel. "The Lord has sent me to tell you these things. Since you did not believe, you will not be able to speak until your son is born." And Gabriel left him.

Zechariah walked outside to the people waiting. "What is wrong with him?" they asked each other. "Why can't he talk?"

Soon the people realized Zechariah had seen a vision.

Later, in a town nearby, Mary worked in her house. She was sweeping the floor when a man in bright clothing suddenly appeared in the room.

"Hello, Mary," said Gabriel. "The Lord has chosen you for a special purpose."

Mary trembled and dropped to her knees at the strange sight of the angel.

"Don't be afraid," said Gabriel. "You will have a son and his name will be Jesus. He will be a great and wonderful person."

"How can this be?" said Mary.

"Everything is possible with the Lord," said Gabriel.

"The Lord will cause your relative, Elizabeth, who could not have children, to have a son also."

"I will serve the Lord," said Mary. Then Gabriel left her.

When Mary heard Elizabeth would have a son, she packed a few items and walked to the town where Zechariah and Elizabeth lived.

Soon Mary saw Elizabeth in the distance, standing outside of her house. Mary waved and Elizabeth waved back. "Hello, Elizabeth."

"So good to see you," said Mary after she ran up to Elizabeth. They hugged.

"The Lord said I am to have a son," said Elizabeth.

"Me, too," said Mary. "Our sons will have a special purpose for serving the Lord,"

"Yes," Elizabeth said, placing her hands on her stomach. "I can already feel the child. When I heard you call my name, the baby leaped for joy inside me. He knows your baby is the Savior."

Mary stayed with Elizabeth for a few months before going home. The time came for Elizabeth to have her baby. Just as the angel had said, the baby was a boy.

"What will his name be?" people asked.

"John," said Zechariah. It was the first time he had spoken since Gabriel's visit. And so the baby's name became John.

Meanwhile, Mary prayed every day in her little house. She thought about the visit of the angel and wondered why the Lord had picked her to be the mother of the Savior.

"Dear Lord," she prayed, "I know with you, all things are possible. I am a little nervous and confused about the things that will happen, but I trust You will protect me and make things work out right."

The Story of

JESUS

Retold by Dandi

For years the world waited, expecting the coming of a Savior. Then a young girl named Mary received a surprise visit from an angel. "God has chosen *you*, Mary," said the angel, "to be the mother of His only son!"

So Mary and Joseph were married. About this time, an order went out demanding that all the Jews travel to their families' hometowns to pay taxes. Mary and Joseph would have to go to Bethlehem. Mary was close to her time to give birth. This long journey was not what she and Joseph had expected.

The journey to Bethlehem was long and rough.

"It will be okay, Mary," Joseph told her as they entered Bethlehem. "I will find a room for you at an inn. You'll have a nice, comfortable place to have the baby."

But Bethlehem was crowded. Every inn Joseph tried turned him down. "No room here!" they said.

Joseph grew anxious for Mary. This was not what he had expected when he brought his wife to Bethlehem.

The last innkeeper told Joseph his inn was full too. But when he saw Mary, he said, "Well, I guess you could stay in the stable."

So in the stable, with the cows and donkeys, and roosters, Joseph made a place for Mary. "I know this is not what you expected," Joseph said.

But Mary smiled at her husband. She knew God would take care of them.

There in the stable, Mary gave birth to the baby Jesus. She wrapped the baby in strips of cloth and laid him in a manger. It was the most important night in the history of the world. Instead of a royal bed of golden cushions, the Savior lay in a bed of straw – not what might be expected for the King of kings.

Out in the countryside, a young shepherd boy expected nothing more than to pass the night as he always did, guarding the sheep from wolves. Poor and unimportant in the world, the shepherd boy never expected to be part of the miraculous night that first Christmas.

Suddenly a light shone in the heavens! The frightened little shepherd boy ran to the other shepherds.

"Don't be afraid," said an angel. "I am bringing you the best news ever! The Savior you have waited for has been born tonight in a manger in Bethlehem!" Then a host of angels joined, singing, "Glory to God in the highest, and peace on earth to all who please God!"

"We must go find the newborn King!" said the little shepherd boy. And he trembled with expectation!

The shepherds ran through the countryside and into the village. They shouted the good news to everyone they met. "The Savior is born!"

The little shepherd boy led the way to the stable in Bethlehem. When they saw the baby Jesus, they knew. Everything was exactly as they had been told by the angels. This truly was the son of God!

Far, far away, wise men began their journey. Kings themselves, they had received a special message that the King of all kings had been born. They didn't know what to expect. They only knew that they had to see this king for themselves. The wise men collected their gifts of gold, frankincense, and myrrh. Then they mounted camels and followed the brightest star in the heavens.

The wise men and the shepherds came to see the Christ Child and found much more than they expected:

'I never could have guessed that God would include me in His great plan for the world,' thought the shepherd boy.

'This Baby is greater than any king, greater than we expected,' thought the wise men.

'Such a marvelous plan!' thought Joseph. 'Only our great God would send His one son to earth as a baby to guide us!'

'I never expected to be so blessed,' thought Mary.

People today are still finding the Christ Child and discovering for themselves that Jesus is much, much more than they could have expected.

JESUS GROWS UP

Retold by Andy Rector

Illustrated by Ben Mahan

After Mary had her baby, she and her new husband, Joseph, went to the temple to show their son to the priests.

When Mary and Joseph walked into the temple, an old man named Simeon came over and took baby Jesus out of Mary's arms.

"The Holy Spirit told me," said Simeon, "that I would live to see the Savior. Today the Spirit told me this baby is the Savior. I have waited many years for this day to happen."

Simeon gave the baby back to Mary and walked away with a smile on his face. Then a woman named Anna walked up to Mary and Joseph.

"This baby is the Savior," said Anna in a loud voice so that all the people nearby heard her. "He is special and will serve the Lord."

As Anna walked away, Joseph and Mary looked at each other. They were amazed at all the things being said about their special baby.

Jesus grew into a wise young boy. Once a year Joseph, Mary and many other friends and relatives, walked down to a town called Jerusalem to worship the Lord in a feast called The Passover. When Jesus was twelve, they took such a trip. Many people walked together down the roads until they reached Jerusalem. After Mary and Joseph celebrated the Feast of the Passover they began to walk home with everyone.

"Where is Jesus?" asked Mary.

"Oh, he is probably walking with his friends," Joseph replied. They searched the crowd, but could not find Jesus.

They looked and looked and finally found Jesus in the temple in Jerusalem. Jesus sat with all the teachers talking with them about the scriptures. The teachers were amazed at his wisdom.

"Jesus," said Mary. "Why are you here? You worried us."

"Didn't you know," Jesus said, "that I had to be in my Father's house?" They didn't understand what he meant.

Jesus grew into a strong and wise man. Mary knew her son had been chosen by the Lord to do special things, but most people in town just thought of Jesus as a nice man.

John, Elizabeth's son and cousin of Jesus, was different. He wore clothing made out of camel's hair and a leather belt. He wandered around the countryside eating locust and wild honey.

"Who is this strange man?" people asked.

"I don't know," said others, "but he has some interesting things to say."

They called him John the Baptist because he would preach to the crowds about God, and baptize people in the water.

One day Jesus walked up to the crowds standing around John the Baptist.

"Here he comes," said John. "It's Jesus, the Savior."

"Baptize me," said Jesus to John.

"But you are the Savior. You don't need to be baptized."

"This is the Lord's will."

So John took Jesus down into the Jordan River and baptized him. As Jesus came out of the water, the sky opened up. A white dove flew down and landed on the shoulder of Jesus.

Suddenly everyone around heard a voice from the sky, "You are my son, whom I love; With you I am well pleased." God had spoken.

THE
GOOD
SAMARITAN

Retold by Dandi

There once lived a man

Who, a long time ago,

Set out on a trip

To the town Jericho.

Then robbers jumped out
And they took all his clothes.
They beat him and left him
Confused, I suppose.

He lay by the side

Of the road that's not paved.

When a priest passed his way,

The man thought, 'I am saved!'

Well, the man raised his head.

"Help me, Sir!" the man cried.

But the priest turned his head

And walked off to the side.

'It's all over,' he thought.

Then, how his hopes soared

When he spotted a rabbi!

He screamed, "Praise the Lord!"

But that rabbi was busy

With plans for the day;

So he just crossed the street

And then hurried away.

One last person chanced by,
The man strained to see.
"Just my luck! A Samaritan –
No help for me!"

"For Samaritans hate me,
And I hate them too.
He will kill me himself
Like Samaritans do!"

But to his great surprise

That Samaritan stayed.

Then he bandaged his wounds

And said, "Don't be afraid."

Next, he lifted the man
To his very own beast,
And he led him to safety
And ordered a feast.

The Samaritan bid

The innkeeper, "Take care.

For this man is my brother.

I'll pay what is fair."

Yes, we all are just neighbors.

Let's all be a friend.

It was Jesus who taught us

This story. The End.

JESUS and LAZARUS

Written by Andy Rector

Illustrated by Ben Mahan

In a little town called Bethany lived two sisters, Mary and Martha, and their brother, Lazarus. Jesus visited the three often. They considered Jesus their best friend.

One day Lazarus became sick.

"I don't think he is going to live much longer," said Martha to Mary.

"Let's send someone to get Jesus," said Mary. "I'm sure he will help Lazarus get better."

Jesus was in another town preaching about God. Suddenly a man ran up to him.

"Jesus!"

"Yes, my friend."

"I am a friend of Mary and Martha. They asked me to come and bring you back to their house. Lazarus is very sick."

"This sickness will not end in death. He has become sick for a reason. This is a way to show the glory of God's power."

But Jesus did not leave right then. He continued to do the Lord's work in the town where he got the message about Lazarus. Two days later he left for Bethany.

By the time Jesus arrived in Bethany, Lazarus had died and had been buried in a tomb for four days.

Martha ran out to greet him. "Jesus, if you had been here, Lazarus would not have died. But I know God will do whatever you ask."

Jesus said, "Your brother will rise again."

Martha did not understand what Jesus meant. "Yes, when we all go to heaven, Lazarus will be there in a new life."

Jesus smiled. "I am the resurrection. Whoever believes in me will live forever. Do you believe in me, Martha?"

"Yes my Lord. I believe you are the Christ."

Martha went into the house to get Mary.

"Jesus is looking for you," said Martha. Mary got up and ran outside to see Jesus. Friends and neighbors had

stopped by to comfort Martha and Mary. When they saw Mary running outside, they followed her.

Mary cried. Jesus saw all the friends of Lazarus crying and this made him sad. He cried also.

"Where is the body of Lazarus?" asked Jesus.

Mary and Martha led Jesus to the tomb where the body of Lazarus lay.

"Remove the stone," said Jesus.

"The glory of God will be shown through the death of Lazarus," said Jesus. The stone was moved. Jesus spoke in a loud voice. "Lazarus, come out!"

People gasped. Mary and Martha could not believe it. Lazarus walked out of the tomb. He was alive.

That night Jesus celebrated with Mary, Martha and Lazarus. "We all believe you are the Christ," they said.

THE TRIUMPHAL ENTRY

Retold by Andy Rector

Illustrated by Ben Mahan

One day Jesus and his close friends walked toward a town named Jerusalem. They went there every year at that time to celebrate a feast. Suddenly outside the city gates of Jerusalem, Jesus stopped. He was going to send some of his followers ahead with a job to do.

He said, "Go to the town. You will see a colt tied there, which no one has ridden. Untie it and bring it back to me. If anyone asks you why you are taking the colt, just tell them, 'The Lord needs it.'"

The followers looked surprised, but did as he asked. They ran ahead to find the colt.

The followers went into the city.

"Look," said one of them. "There's a colt tied to the house over there, just like Jesus said."

"How did he know there would be a colt?" asked another.

"Because he's Jesus," said another follower.

They untied the colt. Suddenly two young men walked around the corner.

"What are you doing with our colt?" one of the young men asked.

"The Lord needs it," the followers said.

"Fine," said the young man. "You may borrow it."

The friends of Jesus returned with the colt.

"It was just like you said, Jesus," the followers exclaimed.

Jesus got on the colt and rode into the town of Jerusalem. Many people had come to visit Jerusalem that day for the feast. When the people saw Jesus riding down the middle of the streets of Jerusalem on a colt, they gathered palm branches and began to wave them in the air.

Suddenly the crowd began to chant, "Hosanna! Hosanna!" Others shouted, "Blessed is he who comes in the name of the Lord!"

As Jesus rode the colt through town, the crowds cheered and chanted for a long time. The followers of Jesus became a little nervous.

"What's going on?" one follower asked another. "Why are the people making a fuss over Jesus?"

But none of them knew what to make of the scene.

"The crowd is chanting things from the scriptures," said one of the followers.

"Yes!" said another follower. "They were talking about Jesus!"

One group of men stood behind the crowd and grumbled. They called themselves the Pharisees.

"I've had enough of this Jesus," said a Pharisee. "The people should be paying attention to us, not him."

"I know," said another. "We're the teachers of the scriptures. We should be getting the praise."

So the Pharisees began to think of a way to destroy Jesus.

THE RESURRECTION
of JESUS

Retold by Andy Rector

Illustrated by Ben Mahan

The Pharisees gathered in the dark corners of the temple one evening. They had found a way to destroy Jesus.

"Where is he?" asked one of the Pharisees.

"He said he would be here," said another Pharisee. "Don't worry. He'll be here."

Soon a follower of Jesus, named Judas, walked up to the Pharisees. "I know where Jesus is. If I lead you to him, will you pay me?"

"Yes," said the Pharisees. "Thirty pieces of silver."

"Let's go," said Judas.

The Pharisees and some Roman soldiers followed Judas.

Later that night Jesus and three of his followers, Peter, James, and John, went to the Garden of Gethsemane. "Sit here and pray," said Jesus. "I'm going over there to pray."

Jesus knew that Judas would betray him into the hands of the Pharisees. He came back and found the followers asleep. "Wake up and pray!" said Jesus. He went off to pray again and when he returned he found them asleep again. He woke them up.

Suddenly Judas walked up from the shadows and kissed Jesus. The three followers and Jesus found themselves surrounded by angry Pharisees and soldiers.

The followers became frightened and ran away, leaving Jesus to the hands of the Pharisees and the soldiers.

354

The Pharisees sent Jesus to stand trial before the Roman governor, Pilate. "I don't understand," said Pilate. "What has this man done wrong?"

"He claims to be our king!" cried the Pharisees. "He claims to be God!"

"I don't see him as a bad person," said Pilate, but the crowds screamed for the death of Jesus. "Fine, I will do as you ask," said Pilate.

Soon Jesus was tortured and beaten. The Roman soldiers made him carry a heavy piece of wood up a hill. On that hill they stood the piece of wood up like a pole and nailed the hands and feet of Jesus onto the wood.

Jesus hung from the cross in pain. He said, "Father forgive them for they don't know what they do." Then Jesus died. Some friends of Jesus took his body off the cross and buried him in a cave.

The friends and followers of Jesus missed him. They heard rumors that Jesus lived, but they were not sure what to believe.

One night the close followers of Jesus ate a meal behind locked doors. Suddenly Jesus appeared to them out of nowhere.

"Peace be with you!" said Jesus. The followers could not believe it. Jesus lived. Soon Jesus disappeared again.

Some time later the followers were out fishing one morning. Suddenly Jesus joined them on the beach. They had seen Jesus die with their own eyes, and yet here he was with them again.

"Lord," they said to Jesus, "we are sorry for running 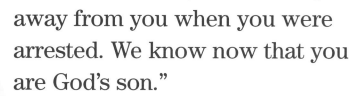 away from you when you were arrested. We know now that you are God's son."

"You are forgiven," said Jesus. And so the followers had breakfast with Jesus that morning on the beach.

The New Testament